to do this Right

POEMS OF FAITH

Second Edition

Rachel Lulich

Copyright © 2018 by Rachel Lulich

Cover Design by Hillary Manton Lodge Design

All Scripture quotations in this publication are taken from the Holy Bible, King James Version (KJV).

All rights reserved. No part of this publication may be reproduced or transmitted in any form or by any means, electronic or mechanical, including photocopy, recording, or any information storage and retrieval system, without permission in writing from the author.

Requests for permission to use or make copies of any part of the work should be made to rachel@brokentopediting.com

[1. Poetry–Subjects & Themes–Inspirational & Religious
2. Poetry–Women authors]

Printed in the United States of America

ISBN: 1985213397
ISBN-13: 978198521339

Dedication

For My Family –

Dad, for teaching me good sense and work ethic.
Mom, for teaching me creativity and spontaneity.
Steven, for teaching me to think and analyze.
Meredith, for adding a peaceful joy to our family.
Ben, for teaching me to recognize and enjoy art.
Saisai, for adding new perspectives to our family.

Second Edition

The second edition of *To Do This Right* features new cover and interior designs, and eight new poems. Other sections, including the dedication, acknowledgements, and about the author content, have also been updated.

List of new poems:

Faithfulness
Oh, Gracious God
Lovingkindness
In Peace
Lay Aside Every Weight
I'm Trying
Good News
Isaiah 65

Contents

PRAYERS AND PRAISES

All My Hope	3
Confessions	4
Amen	5
What Have I Done?	6
Impatience	7
As We Converse	8
Waiting on the Lord	9
Waiting Again	10
Surrender	11
Lamentation	12
Promises	13
Set Free	14
Amazing God	15
To Do This Right	17
Faithfulness	18
Oh, Gracious God	19

CALLING

Here I Am	23
Direction	25
Mixed Signals	26
When I Can't Sleep	27
Compassion	29
Without Words	33
Heaven and Hell	34
Convicted	35

Are You Hearing This?	36
When God Calls	37
Reluctance	38
Lovingkindness	39
For You	40
In Peace	41
Lay Aside Every Weight	42

Musings

The Poet's Heart	45
Trying to Formulate Thought	46
Time	47
Another Pause	48
Drones	49
Drums	51
Heaven Forbid	52
All Things	53
Soul Searching	54
Revival	61
Looking Back	62
I'm Trying	63

Mystery

Listen	67
Good News	68
Faith	69
You Are the Poem	70
Intangible	71
Art	72

How Is It?	73
Without Number	74
Rest on a Promise	75
Our God	76
Still, Small Voice	77
Patience	78
Security	79
Insincere	80
Isaiah 65	81
Mysterious Ways	82
Wonder	83
Communion	84

Acknowledgments

Prayers and Praises

Is any among you afflicted? Let him pray.
Is any merry? Let him sing psalms.

JAMES 5:13

All My Hope

Since all my hope in Christ is found
And all my joy in Jesus,
The more I die to self, I know,
The more he in me liveth.
And though that cross be hard to bear
And though I fall and stumble,
The Lord in me my burden lifts
And for a while I'm humble.

And when I go back to my ways,
Just as I knew I would,
The Lord is gracious to the end
And turns my heart to good.
And when forgetting whom to praise
I start to worship Me,
The Lord in love stands in my way
Till he is all I see.

Then falling at his feet I pray,
Repenting in my shame;
He lifts my head and crowns me still
With peace I cannot claim.
And so I raise my voice in song,
Rejoicing in his will,
And leaving mine behind I learn
That Jesus liveth still.

Confessions

Do I think and do I feel,
Or do I just pretend?
Is this a wheel within a wheel,
Or else world without end?

And am I only using you
To reach what I would gain?
Or is this just the disconnect
Of holy and profane?

How can you stand to look at me?
How can you bear my voice?
And did you hang upon the cross
So I could now rejoice?

Lord, your law is in my heart,
But I am still unclean.
You've called me to a life apart
I couldn't have foreseen.

My head bows in humility,
For what else can I do?
I took the task you gave to me
And put it back on you.

Yet still you lead me out in love
With gentle tenderness;
Your Spirit comes to soothe my soul
While helping me confess.

Amen

Lord, you know I'm fickle;
My will is made of brass.
I ask to race then ask for grace
To let the runners pass:

My soul ran fast to meet you;
Too soon my courage failed.
I asked for freedom from my cross,
Unwilling to be nailed.

Lord, you know I'm sorry;
I long to serve you well.
No matter what I think or pray,
Continue to compel.

What Have I Done?

Why do you bother? Why bother with me?
What have I done to gain your sight?
I sit on my laurels; I sit on my heels,
Ignoring every call to fight.

Why are you patient? Why forbear?
What have I done to gain such grace?
I stand with my back up, defiant in pride
Resisting the knowledge of my shame.

But Lord, you are more wonderful
Than we can hope to understand:
Praise God, from whom all blessing flow,
Who suffered death on our behalf.

Impatience

Lord, can I have an audience?
I have a few questions to ask:
I'm wondering why you made me like this,
And for what specific task.

Give me a vision of what lies in store,
Then give me the courage to face it.
I know I'm not ready, but we never are,
So I ask for your strength in my spirit.

Am I impatient? Probably.
Last time I quaked in fear.
But I recovered with your peace
And felt your spirit near.

I thank you for that time of peace;
I thank you for your grace.
Now touch my soul with living coals
Before I see your face.

I ask you, Lord, to send me –
Give all that I can bear,
Although I scarce can breathe for fear
You'll answer my own prayer.

As We Converse

Am I ready for anything?
I cannot answer that.
The answer's no; it should be yes
Without one caveat.

I am a coward in my bones;
Of this you are aware.
So why did you lay on my heart
Desire, to ensnare?

You've outmaneuvered all excuse
By using my own verse;
I must acknowledge and concede
Your point as we converse.

So how do I commit to what
I fear and cannot see?
I worry what you send my way
May be the end of me.

Lord, I don't know how to die
And rise up from the ashes.
Please handle me with gentle care
Now, as my soul abashes.

Take my very life, oh Lord,
To do with what you will.
Withhold no good thing from me now,
As I try to be still.

Waiting on the Lord

Lord, you know I have things on my mind;
My head and heart are so weighed down.
I'm trying to discern what I should do,
But end up turning all around.

I know you're with me every day and night
And I don't need to be afraid,
But that won't stop desire to do things right,
And you know I find it hard to wait.

You give me peace when I am truly still,
So I will learn to rest in you.
And although others clamor in my ear
I'll cling to what I know is true.

I try to keep in mind all that you've done –
Why is it so hard to believe
That God, who sacrificed his only Son,
Will hold back nothing that we need?

Waiting Again

Here I am again, Lord –
Again and again and again.
I keep coming back; I can't get away,
So here I am once again.

I asked you "what next" again, Lord,
And again you told me to wait.
But wait for what? I want to know
So I can try to obey.

But I know it's not up to me
To figure everything out.
Your plan will unfold perfectly
Without me bringing it about.

So here I am again, Lord,
Laying the same burdens down.
"To a land I'll show you" is future tense,
And must suffice for now.

Surrender

Lord, I'm all worn out.
Is it from wrestling you?
I've made quite a tidy life
Of resisting the Spirit's pull.
My muscles are trembling and weary;
My chest constrains my lungs.
I worry I'll prevail now,
As in the past I've done.
I like the stale protection
Complacency has brought,
But I know I need more
To be used as I ought.
Son of David, have mercy on me –
Touch my eyes that I may see.

Lamentation

I have called out to God in the night;
I have sought him as the new sun rose;
I have salted my prayers with tears,
Sweetened by the God who knows.

I've forsaken the comfort of friends
And hidden myself with the Lord;
I have searched out a quiet place
And looked for peace in his word.

I have poured out my heart like water;
Upon his name I cried.
He heard my prayer from the depths
And reached across the great divide.

Promises

I surrender all –
All my hopes and dreams;
All my plans and brainstormed answers
To visions I have seen.

I'll give up my life,
And vain attempts to know.
I cannot divine my future
But I don't walk alone.

Make me bold for you –
Give me courage, Lord.
Strengthen me with power in weakness
While your plan unfolds.

Set Free

I cannot write the poem I want –
I've tried it several times,
And each attempt leaves me unsure
Of what I can't describe.

The Lord has healed where I was sick
In ways I can't ignore.
He cleansed my heart with body and blood
So I can sin no more.

Oh, to be saved! I never knew
How wonderful it feels.
The faith so long suppressed set free
Now finally seems real.

Amazing God

I've soared through clouds
Above the peaks of mountains;
Into the sun, and far beneath the moon.
I've seen the lakes;
The rapid glacial rivers
And felt the wind play out its mournful tune.

And thou, oh Lord,
Hast made all that I see -
Amazing God! Amazing God!

The earth below -
The sky stretched wide above me -
As in God's hands I traverse through the air.
The thrill of fear,
But more the joy of being,
Fills up my heart, to worship one so fair.

And thou, oh Lord,
Art worthy of all praise -
Amazing God! Amazing God!

When you came down,
The hearts of men to vanquish,
And lived and died to take away our sin,
You called us 'friend'
And made us brothers with you,
That on our cross we might be born again.

And thou, oh Lord,
Hast given all to me -
Amazing God! Amazing God!

Before I die
And leave this world of anger
To spend my days in peace within your realm,
I'll sing of you
And of the life you gave me,
Till darkness comes and finally overwhelms.

And thou, oh Lord,
I'll praise for all my days -
Amazing God! Amazing God!

To Do This Right

We're on a journey, you and I,
I don't know where, I don't know why;
I'm not quite sure how I'll get by,
So on your word I will rely.

You put my name into the race
And I am trying to keep pace
With all the changes that I face,
But right now I'm in need of grace;

Can we slow down a little bit?
I promise I'm not trying to quit.
The spirit's willing, but I admit
That I was not prepared to sprint.

You said you'd give my heart's desire
And set my soul on living fire.
Did you know then how soon I'd tire
When I saw what that might require?

I need your cloud when days are light;
I need your fire in the night;
I need a star that's more than bright;
I need your strength to do this right.

Faithfulness

Why am I walking alone in this cavern?
Even your presence seems so far away.
I see the signs that you've carved to direct me,
But my faith's flickering, as I delay.

I am not troubled, for I know you're here.
You have ordained it, and it will be so.
I can't help wondering where we are going,
But all you tell me is, "Step out and go."

I have been learning to trust through surrender,
Leaving contingency planning to you.
All I can do is press on and be faithful;
You'll lead and guide me as I wait for you.

So I will praise you, Lord, out of this chaos;
Your Spirit's moving in ways I can't see.
I will surrender my need to be sovereign
In the assurance that you'll care for me.

Oh, Gracious God

Oh Lord, my God – my Comforter –
Your yoke is light, and I am free
From all the pressures of this world
I didn't know I carried.

Your name is love, your word is holy,
So I bow down at your feet.
I find my rest in who you made me,
From who I thought I should be.

Oh, gracious God! I will remember
What you did for me today;
I know my place – I know my role,
And I will trust and obey.

I wandered far in search of something
I didn't need or even want.
You let me see that I am nothing
So I could listen as I ought.

You led me back into the famine
To the first altar I built
And gave me there what I had longed for,
And swept away all my guilt.

Oh, gracious God! I will remember
What you did for me today;
I know my place – I know my role,
And I will trust and obey.

Calling

But the Lord said unto me, Say not, I am a child: for thou shalt go to all that I shall send thee, and whatsoever I command thee thou shalt speak.

JEREMIAH 1:7

Here I Am

Here I am, Lord: send me -
I have prayed these words out loud,
Though I don't know what they mean
And their end cannot be seen.
And though obscured by fog,
I will trust in you, my God.

Consecrate my life to thee -
I have thought within my soul.
But I find I can't let go,
Though you had it long ago.
My whole life I've longed for you –
Tell me what I need to do.

Stay the course and run the race -
You have always said to me,
Every time I have been tried;
Every time I've turned aside.
Give me talents to invest,
Lord, and do not let me rest.

Not my will, but thine be done
Here on earth, as up above.
I'll submit, Lord, to your grace
Knowing I will see your face.
How can this great mystery be,
That we'll share eternity?

On that day I'll be with you,
Yes, I know this to be true.
My long road will finally cease,
And then I will rest in peace.
But till then, I make my plea:
Here I am, Lord: send me.

Direction

Where is it that you want me, Lord?
Or should I just stay here?
Why give me then a heart that burns
The more each passing year?

I'm on the path you put me on,
Trying to reconcile
The feeling that I'm constantly
Forgetting my own denial.

Mixed Signals

Go left, go right,
Go straight, now turn,
Now wait and yield;
Try to discern.

Go up, go down,
Come here, go there,
Go on, come back,
Don't fear, beware.

Look here, look there,
Watch all around,
First slow, then fast,
Now make no sound.

    Just up ahead
    Let's stop a bit;
    I'll stretch my legs
    And recommit.

    Now time to go,
    Or so I thought,
    But I seem stuck
    In 'I cannot'.

When I Can't Sleep

The time goes by silently
As I lie in bed
My thoughts go on constantly
Inside my head
And I wonder why God gave me
All these weights upon my heart
When I have to be up early
As the new day starts.

His ways are incomparable,
His methods unique;
Who else can make possible
What we cannot think?
How he chooses the poor and lowly
Just to show he needs no aide;
He can make our crude works holy
As to dust we fade.

Perhaps there's a plan in store
I can't even guess,
Perhaps I already know
But I won't confess,
And it seems so incredible
And I can't get it through my head,
That the God who breathed the Bible
Should want my words read.

Though I doubt my gift's real value
And I don't know where I should go,
I will trust the Lord anew
With the things I don't know.
And the time I thought I was waiting
Is just the time I should have spent,
And each day our light is fading,
For we've all been sent.

Compassion

I.

At first you only stared at me,
Squinting in the sun.
You looked so small and vulnerable,
And so my heart was won.

I used to write sporadically;
I wish I'd understood
How letters, cards and photographs
Could affect such good.

And now you're standing tall and straight
And smiling bright and broad;
You're growing up to be a man
And learning about God.

I pray you'll follow after him;
I pray he'll bless and keep you.
I pray he'll save you and your house,
And bring you safely through.

II.

Your stature is small, your eyes are wide,
And I wonder what you feel inside.
Is there hope? Is there fear?
Does it seem that nothing's clear?

How shall I communicate
With Evil standing at the gate?
God's power overcomes man's hate,
And his love for you is very great.

I pray he'll speak into your heart
And help you overcome the dark.
I pray your family, too, will see
That Jesus died for you and me.

And when you've grown into a man,
I know already there's a plan
To bless and keep you on your way
To heaven's door, and Glory's day.

III.

We're strangers right now, you and I,
But not for long, I hope.
We'll trade our letters over time,
And friendship will slowly grow.

I pray I can encourage you,
Though from a different life;
I pray my words will help you live
In the midst of strife.

I wish that I could lighten your load,
But I can't remove your cares.
So put your faith in Jesus Christ,
Who listens to your prayers.

IV.

I saw your face and paused.
I couldn't tell you why,
But I knew from the very start
That you were mine.

You'd waited for so long,
And I wondered how it felt
To wait in patience, keeping faith –
What doubts you've quelled.

I pray you'll grow up brave,
Not ever backing down,
Believing fiercely in the Lord
While love abounds.

I'm proud of you already,
And I pray that you'll seek God.
May his blessings be upon you now,
With angelic guard.

Without Words

I bought a woman a sandwich.
(Why didn't I buy her two?)
I gave her the bag and said goodnight,
But I said nothing of you.

I gave a man a banknote
And took his shaking hand;
He said "God bless;" I said the same
And hoped he'd understand.

I'm not so good at small talk -
No gifted evangelist.
Please tell them, Lord, what I did not;
Redeem the chance I missed.

Heaven and Hell

I've heard that growing up is hard
And I won't disagree,
But surely growing wise is worse,
Or so it seems to me.

And as I learn, I start to feel
A little bit afraid –
It seems like God is nudging me
Toward something I've delayed.

I've worried that a time would come
When God would call me out.
Yet I have hoped, despite my fear,
That it would come about.

I've hoped he has some splendid thing,
Some battle I must fight,
And yet I dared not pray for it
For fear perhaps he might.

I pray sincerely from my heart
But I don't mean a word.
I listen to him earnestly
And don't know what I've heard.

What can I do? What can I say?
I don't know who I am.
I don't know what you want from me.
I don't know if I can.

Convicted

We sent out a message,
We asked for your prayers –
Our churches were being burned.
We held our dead elders,
We mourned our dead children,
But from everything we've heard,
You didn't pray for us.

We begged for assistance,
We needed your help –
Our pastors were being jailed.
We gathered in secret,
We whispered in fear,
But from all that we can tell,
You never prayed for us.

We Facebooked and Tweeted,
We emailed and called –
We know the word got out.
We died for a Bible,
We starved for a song,
And yet we had our doubts
That you would pray for us.

Are You Hearing This?

Why do I write?
What do I say?
Are you hearing me?
Tell me what these words are for –
Tell me what they mean.

I cry to the darkness,
Into the void,
Is no one listening?
I try to show what I can't know
Of things I haven't seen.

May God forgive
My unskilled use
Of what he's given me,
And fill the gaps I can't erase
With his eternity.

When God Calls

When God called Abram from his home,
He didn't tell him where.
Did he debate North, East, South, West?
Did he wonder which was best?

When God called Philip to go forth,
He didn't tell him why.
Did he have doubts along the way?
Did he ask him when he prayed?

When God calls us to serve his Son,
He might not tell us how.
Will we demand to see ahead?
Will we overcome our dread?
Will we embrace all that he said?
Do we believe he'll raise the dead?

Reluctance

Lord, you know I'm only me –
You know my heart of hearts.
I'm sure I can't complete the task
Before I even start.

I've told you that I'm slow of tongue
And don't know what to say.
I cannot speak; I am too young;
Perhaps we should delay.

Lord, you know I feel the weight
You've placed upon my back.
You know how much I truly miss
The qualities I lack.

And I get tired and want to shirk,
Avoiding these unknowns,
But you have called me to this work;
Place fire in my bones.

Lovingkindness

I've been obsessed with the silliest dreams –
    the stupidest schemes
      the most harmful things.

I've been engrossed in the life without pattern –
    the noise and the clatter
      of things that don't matter.

But I've been awakening to all my excuses –
    the mythical muses
      and insincere truces.

And I've been attempting to wait and be faithful –
    lay down what I long for
      to rest and be thankful.

I'm finally starting to step out in blindness –
    your song in the silence
      evokes lovingkindness.

For You

Remind me why I'm doing this, Lord;
Increase my efforts in grace.
I lack zeal and focus to follow through,
And I'm constantly saving face.

Help me remember that it's not me
Who called me to do this now.
I sin against you – not just myself,
When I decline your power.

Both God and Mammon – I've heard of that,
But now I'm starting to see.
This can become mere profession,
But it must never be.

A ministry of words – that's what I said,
And that's what I must believe.
For my own sake it's empty, returning void,
But for you, Lord?
                        For you, I can dream.

In Peace

In peace I will lie down and sleep,
But peace feels far away,
And I don't know how I have walked
So long on feet of clay.

They're crumbling beneath me now,
Refusing to convey
My soul of lead another inch
Along my chosen way.

I curse them but I bless them too;
I know who they obey.
I close my eyes and find that I've
Forgotten how to pray.

I ran from all you have for me –
I led myself astray –
Pursuing any vanity
That might keep me away.

So now you've stopped me in my tracks
To hear what you would say.
Restore my trust and I will turn
To meet you on the waves.

Lay Aside Every Weight

I promised you I'd list them out
And try not to deny
The power they have over me,
Increased with every high.

I've already laid some aside,
But I would quit them all -
A sacrifice of Pleasure-domes
That held me so enthralled.

I think you have prepared my heart.
I don't want to be wrong –
Lord, loose my bonds enough to flee
The screaming Siren's song.

Musings

*For God hath not given us the spirit of fear;
but of power, and of love, and of a sound mind.*

2 Timothy 1:7

The Poet's Heart

I wish that I could learn to write
Like the poets did of old,
To warm the hearts of all who fight
For heaven's crowns of gold.

I wish my pen would burn for me,
Producing words of flame,
To tell of things I cannot see,
And joys I couldn't name.

But God can use imperfect skill,
So I don't write in vain.
My words are bended to his will
To glorify his name.

Trying to Formulate Thought

I'm searching for something, I don't know what;
I'm trying to formulate thought.
I'm keeping too busy to sit and reflect,
And lessons from you are unsought.

Why such surprise, then, when nothing occurs
To quicken my heart or mind?
How can I hope to be of use
With no time for thinking assigned?

Time

I have no time
My life is so rushed:
There's no time for reading,
Writing and such.

If you'll forgive me,
I'll skip church today;
I won't read your words,
Or make time to pray.

Each moment's a choice
To fit God in;
Each day is a challenge
To hear through the din.

My life is God's,
So why do I spend it
Doing what I want
And trying to defend it?

God and I –
That should come first.
But it rarely seems to,
And so I still thirst.

Another Pause

So why another dry spell? Why another pause?
I had a spurt of growth, now momentum's gone.
I felt my spirit stirring; I felt the pull of God;
I had a sort of vision of the road I'm on.

You stoked the coals within me; you nudged me from behind;
You spoke to me so clearly, I could have no doubt.
And now I sit here reaching; now I'm in the dark.
Would you deny me water at the edge of drought?

I felt my heart surrender; I felt my soul give in;
My mind and spirit trembled, but something in me burned.
And now emotion's left me; my love is once more cold.
How quickly I've discarded all the things I've learned.

Drones

We're marching, marching, marching through life
Not looking to the left or right
And we can't see above the shoulders
Of those in front, who also have no sight.

We're walking, walking, with precision
Trying to avoid the fight
Denying our own indecision
Insisting, no exceptions, we're alright.

And they're all watching as we go,
Not lambs to the slaughter, we;
We're more worried about skin than soul;
Of here and now, than mere eternity.

So when they tell us, "Bow and pray,"
No Shadracks, Meshacks, Abednigos
Refuse compliance with their demand;
For we esteem the power of our foes.

We're tramping, tramping, tramping along
Only going where we're told.
Hardly caring for the truth,
We pretend to take our orders from the Lord.

We're slogging, slogging, through the world
Despondent and bent down and beaten; abused.
And they all sneer at our despair
And our terrified gasps each time our heels are bruised.

We're playing at soldiers, pretending we're brave,
But we'd rather fit in than be set apart.
No one's immune to pain or fear,
But compromise can only stretch so far.

"I may not be perfect, but I'm not that bad."
"I'm okay without it." "I'm fine as I am."
These are the lies that we turn to for comfort,
Rejecting our prodigal nature to be damned.

We're stepping, stepping, stepping with caution,
Ashamed to go back and turn ourselves in.
Pride trumping sense, we go on as we are,
Embracing the seas of despair once again, and again.

Drums

The drums of revolt beat louder each day;
The rhythms of anarchy pulsing.
The trumpet-notes blare with each victory
And volume is all their rejoicing.

They cried "Persecution!" and now persecute,
No contrary thoughts tolerated.
They laid on the pressure by calling it 'progress;'
The baffled Church capitulated.

Perhaps, after all, we've been a bit harsh –
Perhaps presentation should change.
And this and that doctrine don't sound very nice,
So we'll soften them, lest we estrange.

The false analogy's alive and well,
Telling us it's all the same.
We can't love the sinner and still hate the sin -
"They're one now," our pastors proclaim.

Who stands in the gap and weeps for the nation?
Who prays for a Jonah to come?
I can't hear their voices above the great noise
Of our own, who have picked up their drums.

Heaven Forbid

Heaven forbid we're pedantic;
Heaven forbid we speak up.
Nobody wants to hear "Listen."
Nobody wants to be changed.

Why can we no longer handle
Critique that's for our own good?
Is that why we don't read our Bibles –
Lest our lives be rearranged?

Where did this watery faith come from?
Where this self-centered life?
How long before we're scattered,
Left choking on our pride?

Since when are we willing to risk it –
That fiery wrath of our God?
Since when do we no longer fear him
From whom we can never hide?

All Things

All my thoughts and energies
Are bending to this life.
I try to leave them here with you,
Yet somehow they survive.

All my desires and every wish
Would serve the will of God.
My heart and soul would please, and yet,
I don't do as I ought.

I have idols, though not of gold,
I should tear down, but don't.
I know changes I should make,
But usually won't.

All my plans to serve are weak,
Forgetting all your power,
And I have never dared dream big,
Or sought my 'finest hour.'

Now I'm venturing to trust
And inching to the ledge,
But I still test each step with care,
Unwilling to find the edge.

Soul Searching

I.

When asked, I answer easily;
My weaknesses are few,
And all are turning into strengths
As is, of course, my due.
I analyze each question posed
And think before I speak,
Then eloquently justify
And say my spirit's meek.
But you question everything I say
And make me realize
I wasn't searching deep enough,
And couldn't see the lies.
So now the real soul searching has to start
As I confront the shadows of my heart.

II.

Not too deep! Although I look myself,
What lies within my heart is there to stay;
Just small glimpses, occasionally shared,
Are set to paper in my metered way.
Beyond my art I rarely share such thoughts,
Even when I close my eyes in prayer
Unless the Lord insists till I give in,
So how can I tell others, who'll forbear?
At times I wish I'd just come out and say
(Without reserve or stalling for more time)
The thoughts and truths I bury in my soul,
But it's so hard to admit the sins I find.
I want to say aloud that which I write,
But the silence is too strong to fight.

III.

I can rest easy knowing God made me –
Knowing he'll change me at his own pace,
Chipping away till he leaves not a trace
Of the old person I used to be.
I can relax as I wait for his timing,
Wait for convictions to really sink in.
I know he'll accomplish all he begins,
But pretend there's no flame in the work of refining.
What an excuse to sit idly by
Denying my role in being sanctified.
Lord, "mold me and make me," I've often prayed,
But rather than yield, I've resisted; delayed.
It's time to start working – to roll up my sleeves:
Lord give me the strength to go to my knees.

IV.

I can't go on – it's far too hard;
I can't be vulnerable.
Too used, perhaps, to being strong,
I can't be vulnerable.
I won't go on – my stomach churns
And I can't spit out the words.
Too used, perhaps, to silent thought,
I can't spit out the words.
Why within me such unrest?
Why do I always try to suppress?
I need to speak, and yet I can't –
The struggle tortures me.
Just shove me, Lord, or I won't act,
Even to be free.

V.

Share all this? Insanity.
It's far too close to me.
I know I vowed to open up,
But not to this degree;
Don't I decide what I should tell
Of what I think and feel?
It's my right to keep it all
Just surface-level real.
You think you've come to know me?
You think you're digging deep?
You've barely scratched the surface –
Still waters still run deep;
You've no idea how much goes on
Beyond the boundary I have drawn.

VI.

No more! I'm tired of holding back
And fidgeting in fear.
I'll boldly face the throne of grace
And seek God's mercy there.
Transparency will be my goal
Although it's hard for me –
I'll trust the Lord to pair my words
With opportunity.
God uses iron to sharpen iron
And fire to refine,
So comfort is the great deceit
That I need to deny.
Perhaps this turmoil is my cross
To take and follow Christ.

VII.

I know I'll never reach perfection here,
But I can strive to walk at Jesus' side;
Although it's hard for me to remain near,
I long to do what makes him glorified.
So I'm resolved again to honesty
And holding back still less than I have done;
Not only search me, Lord, but work in me
And make me more and more like Christ, your Son.
I give this up to you in hope and fear
And wouldn't ever take it back again,
But don't let me forget a single tear
That I have shed for this too-subtle sin.
Bless my efforts, as they are in your name,
And make your glory, Lord, my only aim.

Revival

I'm quite adept at protecting myself,
With fortified walls round my heart;
No one can breach these defenses I've built,
With their 24-hour guard.

But I feel the stir of conviction within –
I've built my watchtowers too sound.
In all of my efforts to close myself in,
I've ended up shutting God out.

I open the gate for him when it looks safe,
But I watch his every move;
Just when I see he has something in mind,
I show him the door and elude.

Why don't I trust him? Why don't I dare?
Is my faith so very weak?
I don't want to get in the boat, for fear
The waves will be too deep.

You have plans for me, I know –
It scares me half to death.
I'd rather stay here and lay low,
But you won't let me rest.

You've put that fire in my bones
That makes my stomach churn,
And every time you stir my soul
I feel its embers burn.

Looking Back

Looking back, I sometimes wish
I did things differently;
My life is jumbled odds and ends
Linked together haphazardly.

Looking back at what I've done
Sometimes I have to wonder:
Would I have accomplished more
If I had started sooner?

But I'd turn down a time machine
To change the way things were;
I wouldn't be who I am now
If they had not occurred.

Looking back, I often see
The way God shaped my heart;
The education I've received
Infuses all my art.

I'm Trying

I'm trying – almost crying because I'm dying,
But not to self –
    – I need your help
To escape the sea of sin's diseases
That have infected me.

I'm erring, not quite daring, because I scare
So easily –
    – I'm on my knees
Can't you hear me? Won't you heal me of
My insincerity?

I'm symptomatic, like an addict, so I'm panicked
All the time –
    – I can't align
Myself with Grace, I can't erase my
Missteps in this race.

But Lord

You're loving, overcoming and uncovering
My very soul –
    – I should have known
You wouldn't stop until my thoughts were
Bending toward you as they ought.

Mystery

*Such knowledge is too wonderful for me;
it is high, I cannot attain unto it.*

PSALM 139:6

Listen

Listen to the silence
In the chaos of your soul;
Listen to the beauty
Of the parts making the whole.

Listen to the echo
In the hollow place within;
Listen to the goodness
That overcomes the din.

Listen to the voices
In the prison of our times;
Listen to the justice
And answer for our crimes.

Listen to the rhythm
In consciences that sway;
Listen to the mercy
That takes us anyway.

Listen to the music
In the quiet of the night;
Listen to the glory
Of unknowable delight.

Listen to the breathing
In the stillness of the earth;
And listen to the mystery
Of undeserving worth.

Good News

The Christmas hymns have all been sung;
The presents are under the tree,
Reminding us that wise men gave
Their gifts on bended knee.

"Fear not," the angel said, and told
The shepherds in the night,
That Christ was born in Bethlehem
To set the world aright.

So God was laid in a manger,
Made low for all to see.
He lived to die on a wretched cross
To make the sinner free.

And now, ascended in glory,
Forgiving our endless sin,
The Lord of all will return one day,
And all will worship him.

Faith

Man of Sorrows, what a name;
I can't even begin
To understand just what it means
To die for someone's sin.

And if that's hard to comprehend,
Then how can I expect
To wrap my head around the fact
That Jesus conquered death?

My knowledge is so incomplete –
The veil is still in place.
But faith steps in to fill the gaps
In evidence of grace.

You Are the Poem

You are the poem I can almost write,
The portrait I cannot paint,
You're in the receding evening light
When everything seems faint.

Your grace fills shadows beneath the sun
And diffusions of light at dusk.
If I tried to describe you, I'd be undone;
Our best efforts are never enough.

Intangible

There will never be a line of verse
That can hope to measure up
To the feelings in a poet's soul
In a quiet time with God.

There will never be a melody
That's quite as sweet and clear
As the joy in the musician's heart
When worshipping the Lord.

There will never be a piece of art
That fully represents
The awe and wonder of this world
That God spoke into being.

There will never be a quiet prayer
Earnest and humble enough
To match the gratitude that's felt
When reflecting on his love.

And there will never be a thing
That we can ever do
To deserve the heavenly grace
He offers us each day.

Art

What is a poet? I couldn't say –
Only God can know.
What is it makes us slaves to words,
These seeds we try to sow?

What is a painter? Who can guess?
Who can understand
How art, with no linguistic aides,
Can help us comprehend?

What are musicians? Why can they
Stir up within our souls
Such deep response to harmony,
Unveiling the unknown?

What is an artist? Who can say?
Only God above
Can fully understand the act
Of creating works in love.

How is it?

How is it, Lord, that you exist
And made all that I see?
How is it that I know you are,
And that you live in me?

Often, it seems, I don't even care
About who you really are;
I don't know what to make of the fact
That God is a consuming fire.

And how, Lord, does it even work,
When you speak to me?
I've read your words since I was young,
And still there's more to see.

Often, it seems, I don't understand
Things I've learned from afar,
But you, who are omnipotent,
Continue to inspire.

Without Number

How precious are your thoughts to me,
Outnumbering the sand.
Will you send angels for my words
As I try to understand?

There are countless brands of faith,
But only one true God
Existing in a Trinity
Of spirit, law and blood.

We aim, and daily miss the mark,
But still you guide our steps.
And though we are of little faith,
Each small attempt is blessed.

Rest on a Promise

'Greatly beloved' and 'Friend of God';
'A man after God's own heart'.
How grand those titles sound to me,
That set these men apart.

Were they perfect? Heavens, no -
Their natures just like mine.
But they sought God faithfully,
Pursuing the Divine.

Nowadays, we doubt he'll do
Great deeds, as in the past,
But even now in every life
He works before he's asked.

God's promises are made to all;
We can lie down in peace
And watch the angels, up and down,
In Jacob's Ladder dreams.

Our God

Our God is not a trickster god -
He doesn't lead astray.
We can walk in faith with him,
For even death is gain.

So when he sets a test for us
Or gives us trials to bear,
We can hope and wait and watch
To find his good things there.

And all our joy will be in him
And following his will:
When we go out, led forth with peace,
The trees just won't be still.

Still, Small Voice

We say "God's voice is still and small,"
Like he can be ignored,
Implying that he has no power
To say "arise, and go."

As if, because it's small, it cannot
Breach our crowded minds.
But how, then, can his voice convict,
Exposing all our lies?

Our connotations miss the mark,
Suppressed in doubt and fear,
But I've never known a voice as strong
As the one I cannot hear.

Patience

I know the Lord has heard me –
I sense his presence in me,
But I can't quite describe it
Or hold its power and grace in my own hands.

So I will climb my tower
And stand the watch assigned me,
And I will wait and listen
To see what God has written in the sand.

And I know I'm not abandoned –
I hear his questions to me,
And I know I must answer
And willingly do all that he commands.

For God will work such wonders,
That even if he told me,
Yet I could not believe it;
I'll wonder at his wrath upon the land.

And so I pray: Revive us –
In wrath remember mercy.
And though the trees don't blossom,
I'll praise God for the future he has planned.

Security

Trusting the Lord with all your heart
Isn't so easy to do.
"It's not hard to find answers – they're hard to accept"
Never rang so true.

And seeking first the kingdom of God
Gets muddled with 'all these things'.
So I give unto Caesar and keep for myself,
And the promise is never redeemed.

Insincere

I worry this will become a lie,
A 'living' that I make.
Will my work be strained and stiff,
And altogether fake?

I know that I can't seize control
If I want to stay sincere.
My motives must find root in faith,
Avoiding sands of fear.

No 'trying' then – I can't succeed
By writing on my own.
Only God can make this work –
Without him, I will fail.

Isaiah 65

We didn't ask for you today –
We sat among the graves;
Said once again, "keep to yourself"
And wandered, unafraid.

We walked after our empty thoughts,
A sacrifice of smoke.
We didn't answer when you called
Or listen when you spoke.

But Lord, you'll lure us back in,
Surprising with your nearness,
Employing all that speaks to us;
Conviction with a promise:

We will remember what we forgot –
Before we call, you'll answer.
While we're yet speaking, you will hear –
Our God and Priest and Master.

Mysterious Ways

Am I tiring to you, Lord,
With constant fall and need?
Is it alright to use my time
With you, mostly to plead?

I praise you when I see your work
And answers to my prayers;
You have absorbed my every load
And lightened all my cares.

Do you take pleasure in surprise?
Do you love how we love it?
It's practically your calling card,
This unexpected wit.

I love you, Lord, and all you do
For those who love your name.
You comfort me before the end
Of all this stress and strain
And I'm excited to see how you'll
Redeem it once again.

Wonder

I cannot hide and cannot tell,
Though I have tried them both.
Once the blessings that I sought;
Once me, now him alone.

A burning bush or blackberries?
The distinction can't be made.
Scaffolds of truth surround the lies
He already forgave.

How to give back the life I owe
And spurn blind unbelief?
How to meet Agape's love
With Phileo, causing grief?

God is his own interpreter –
Objective truth in Word.
His wonder colors all I've seen
And everything I've heard.

Communion

Blessed communion, gift of God;
Broken body and out-poured blood.
Convicting grace, forgiven sin;
Now my service can begin.

Acknowledgements

In July 2012, I wrote a poem. I hadn't written any for ages. But God was speaking, and for a change, I was listening. I made a commitment then to self-publish a collection of my poems, and my life has completely changed in the process.

Unending thanks to my gracious family for their unconditional love and for putting up with all my wild brainstorming ideas throughout this sometimes tumultuous process.

I am so grateful to all those who have read various drafts of my poems and of this collection, especially Steven Lulich, Penny Lulich, Mary Cairns, Mike Edsall, Hillary Lodge, Erica Simonson, Janell Teach, and Dana Voth.

I would also like to thank my friends at Grove First Baptist Church for their friendship, enthusiasm and prayers as I compiled the first edition.

Finally, many thanks to my friend Hillary Manton Lodge for redesigning the cover and interior of this second edition, my professors and colleagues at Portland State University, and my wonderful family at Lake Bible Church.

About the Author

Rachel Lulich is a poet and playwright, and blogs about the intersection of art and faith at The Fifth Sola. Led by her love of books to study literature in college, she went on to teach English in China and serve in the United States Air Force before earning her MA in Book Publishing from Portland State University. Lulich is a freelance editor and founder of Broken Top Editing. Her hobbies include travel, foreign languages, and of course, reading.

For more information:

The Fifth Sola – www.5thsola.blogspot.com
Broken Top Editing – www.brokentopediting.com

Trust in the LORD *with all thine heart; and lean not unto thine own understanding. In all thy ways acknowledge him, and he shall direct thy paths.*

PROVERBS 3:5-6

Made in the USA
Columbia, SC
24 November 2022